MONTREAL

PERCY ROWE AND PATIENCE COSTER

WORLD ALMANAC® LIBRARY

Please visit our web site at: www.worldalmanaclibrary.com
For a free color catalog describing World Almanac® Library's list of high-quality books
and multimedia programs, call 1-800-848-2928 (USA) or 1-800-387-3178 (Canada).
World Almanac® Library's fax: (414) 332-3567.

Library of Congress Cataloging-in-Publication Data

Rowe, Percy.
    Montreal / by Percy Rowe and Patience Coster.
        p. cm. — (Great cities of the world)
    Includes bibliographical references and index.
    ISBN 0-8368-5039-4 (lib. bdg.)
    ISBN 0-8368-5199-4 (softcover)
    1. Montrââl (Quâbec)—Juvenile literature. I. Coster, Patience. II. Title.
    III. Series.
    F1054.5.M84R68   2004
    971.4'28—dc22   2004047976

First published in 2005 by
World Almanac® Library
330 West Olive Street, Suite 100
Milwaukee, WI 53212 USA

Copyright © 2005 by World Almanac® Library.

Produced by Discovery Books
Editor: Patience Coster
Series designers: Laurie Shock, Keith Williams
Designer and page production: Keith Williams
Photo researcher: Laura Durman
Maps: Stefan Chabluk
World Almanac® Library editorial direction: Mark J. Sachner
World Almanac® Library editor: Gini Holland
World Almanac® Library art direction: Tammy West
World Almanac® Library graphic design: Scott M. Krall
World Almanac® Library production: Jessica Morris

Photo credits: AKG-Images: p.10; Axiom/Chris Coe: p.28; Bettmann/Corbis: p.14; Chris Fairclough Photography:
pp.24, 29; Corbis/Earl & Nazima Kowall: p.42; Corbis/Kelly-Mooney Photography: p.21; Corbis/Kit Kettle: p.16;
Corbis/Paul A. Souders: pp.8, 43; Corbis/Robert Holmes: p.20; Corbis Sygma/Jacques Langevin: p.34; Hogan Visions
Photography/Kharim Hogan: p.31; Hulton Deutsch Collection/Corbis: p.12; Hutchison/Jackum Brown: p.4; James Davis
Worldwide: p.33; Mary Evans Picture Library: p.9; Parc Jean-Drapeau: p.38; Parc Jean-Drapeau/Sébastien Larose: p.7;
Rachel Jacklyn-Bilodeau http://rachelita.com: pp.30, 37; Reuters: p19; Stéphan Poulin: p.25; Still Pictures/J. C. Teyssier:
p13; Travel Stock Photography/Buddy Mays: p.18; Trip/B. Turner: pp.17, 32, 36; Trip/J. Cherfas: p.39; Trip/T. Bognar:
pp.22, 27, 35, 41

Cover caption: A Montreal street (photograph reproduced by permission of Chris Fairclough Photography).

Printed in the United States of America

1 2 3 4 5 6 7 8 9 08 07 06 05 04

Contents

Introduction

The lively, cosmopolitan city of Montreal is in Quebec, the largest province in Canada. With ancient origins as a Native American settlement, Montreal is Canada's second-largest city (the largest is Toronto). About 45 miles (72 kilometers) north of the U.S. border, Montreal lies on the St. Lawrence River, a huge waterway linking the Atlantic Ocean with the vast inland lakes and forests of Canada and the United States.

The European Influence

From the seventeenth century, Montreal's strategic position 1,000 miles (1,600 km) upriver from the ocean made it an important

◀ *A view of the city of Montreal, looking downtown from the west.*

center for European, particularly French and British, traders and explorers. Today, Montreal is still divided mainly along French and English lines. In the west of the city, English predominates; in the east, French. It is, however, also a multiethnic city, with a wide range of different cultural groups.

Of Canada's population of 33 million people, about one-quarter are French-speaking and of French heritage. Although the French are a minority in Canada, they are a majority in Quebec province. English-speaking people are the majority of the population in Canada, but they are a minority in Quebec. Montreal's population is 70 percent French-speaking, with 15 percent English-speaking residents.

A Rich Culture

Montreal is the third-largest French-speaking city in the world, after Paris in France and Kinshasa, Democratic Republic of the Congo, in Africa. It is a place of good food and drink, with a wealth of bars, cafés, shops, and festivals. Montreal's thriving arts community includes writers, painters, dancers, and musicians.

While French culture predominates—with sidewalk cafés and patisseries selling croissants and brioches—much of the architecture is British influenced. Many residential buildings in Montreal were constructed by Scottish merchants during the nineteenth century. Their fine Victorian houses are similar to those found in Edinburgh, Scotland.

CITY FACTS

Montreal

Founded: 1642

Area (City): 72 square miles (186 square kilometers)

Area (Metropolitan): 1,563 sq mi (4,047 sq km)

Population (City): 1,016,376

Population (Metropolitan): 3,393,739

Population Density (City): 14,116 per sq mi (5,590 per sq km)

Population Density (Metropolitan): 2,171 per sq mi (847 per sq km)

Government in Canada

Canada is a federation, dividing its political power between the central government and its ten provinces. Parliament, elected by the people and composed of a House of Commons and a Senate, meets in Ottawa, the country's capital. The prime minister heads the government. Each province has its local government, headed by a premier.

"The river, flowing past the island on which the city stands, created the highway which made Montreal such a natural center for trade and commerce."

—Aline Gubbay, contemporary urban historian.

Montreal Metropolitan Area

✈ Mirabel International Airport

Montreal
Other built up areas

LAURENTIAN MOUNTAINS

Repentigny

Terrebonne

Rosemere   LAVAL   Varennes

Île Jesus

St.-Eustache

N

Laval   Île de Montreal   Boucherville

Île Bizard   Pierrefonds   Île Sainte-Hélène

Deux-Montagnes Lake   Dorval International Airport   Outremont   Longueuil   Île Notre-Dame

St.-Laurent   MONTREAL   St.-Hubert

Beaconsfield   Dorval   Lachine   Brossard

Île Perrot   La Salle   La Prairie

Châteauguay   St. Lawrence River

miles   0   4
0   4   kilometers

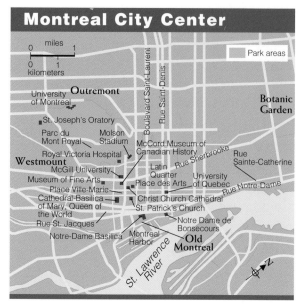

Montreal City Center

miles   0   1
0   1   kilometers

Park areas

University of Montreal   Outremont   Boulevard Saint-Laurent   Rue Saint-Denis   Botanic Garden

St. Joseph's Oratory

Parc du Mont Royal   Molson Stadium   McCord Museum of Canadian History   Rue Sherbrooke   Rue Sainte-Catherine

Royal Victoria Hospital   Latin Quarter   University

Westmount   McGill University   Place des Arts   of Quebec   Rue Notre-Dame

Museum of Fine Arts   Place Ville-Marie   Christ Church Cathedral

Cathedral-Basilica of Mary, Queen of the World   St. Patrick's Church

Rue St. Jacques   Notre Dame de Bonsecours

Notre-Dame Basilica   Montreal Harbor   Old Montreal

St. Lawrence River   N

Like Britain, Canada has a constitutional monarchy. Queen Elizabeth II of Britain is also queen of Canada. She has a permanent representative, the Governor General, in Ottawa, Canada's capital. The mainly French-speaking citizens of Quebec province have, for the past forty years, wanted their state to be independent from Britain. In 1995, a referendum was held proposing independence for Quebec, but it was defeated by a margin of 1.12 percent.

An Island City

Montreal thrives on an island where two major rivers, the St. Lawrence and the Ottawa, meet. The city covers about two-fifths of the island, which is about 32 miles (51 km) long and 10 miles (16 km) wide. Montreal largely owes its existence to the nearby Lachine Rapids, which for centuries prevented ships coming from the Atlantic Ocean from continuing farther upriver. As a result, Montreal became a major port for the

transfer of goods between Canada and countries overseas.

Mont Royal

The island is a flat, fertile expanse of land around a single, tree-covered peak, the 755-foot (230-meter) Mont Royal. Known as "the mountain" by locals, Mont Royal is in the center of the island. Between the river and Mont Royal, the narrow streets of Old Montreal, with its eighteenth- and nineteenth-century buildings, contrast with the skyscraper offices and modern shopping streets that make up downtown. On the green mountainside are the wealthy residential areas of Westmount and Outremont.

A Snowy City

The people of Montreal endure extremely cold winters with night temperatures of 5° Fahrenheit (−15° Centigrade) common

between December and March. The daily average temperature in January is 15° F (−9.5°C), but temperatures can drop as low as −40 °F (−40°C). There may be ten heavy snowfalls, reaching a depth of up to 8 feet (2.5 m). The city has a short spring and the leap between winter and summer can be very abrupt. In summer, the weather is often hot and humid, and temperatures can rise to 90° F (32°C). The daily average temperature for July is 70° F (21°C). Fall brings cooler weather and sunny days, and the city appears at its most beautiful—surrounded by scarlet and gold maple forests.

▲ *Montrealers ride tube slides at the Snow Festival, a fun-filled family event which takes place every year on Île Sainte-Hélène.*

The Unknown City

Quebec's third-largest city, Laval, is situated on another large island in the St. Lawrence River. This island, called Jesus, is joined to Montreal by bridges. Most of Laval's residents work in Montreal. Most Montrealers only pass through Laval on their way to the vacation spot of the Laurentian Mountains.

CHAPTER 1

History of Montreal

In 1535, Jacques Cartier, a sailor and explorer from the town of St. Malo in France, traveled up the St. Lawrence River with a crew of fifty men in a convoy of two ships. He had been sent by King Francis I of France "to discover islands and countries where they say there is a lot of gold." Like many other people at the time, Cartier thought that North America was part of Asia, a land of gold, spices, and silk.

Place of the Beaver

Cartier's progress up the St. Lawrence was halted by river rapids—later named the Lachine (or China) Rapids. He disembarked at an Indian settlement called Hochelaga, meaning, in the Huron (Native American) language, "Place of the Beaver." Cartier planted a cross and claimed the island for

"You are a grain of mustard seed that shall grow till its branches overshadow the earth. You are few, but this work is the Word of God. His smile is on you, and your children shall fill the land."

—Father Vimont, Jesuit priest in Montreal, 1642.

◄ *A statue of Paul de Chomedey, first governor of the island of Montreal in 1642, stands in the middle of the Place d'Armes in downtown.*

his king, naming the hill in its center "Mont Royal" (from which the city eventually took its name). The chief of Hochelaga presented Cartier with gifts for his return journey to France, including a beaver pelt (skin).

Two Fearless Women

In 1644, a young nurse, Jeanne Mance, opened Montreal's first hospital, l'Hôtel Dieu. In 1671, a teacher, Marguerite Bourgeoys, founded the first chapel, Notre Dame de Bonsecours ("Our Lady of Divine Assistance"). Rebuilt in 1772, the second chapel, with the same name, still stands. Both women were frail; Mance had nearly died during the Atlantic crossing to Canada. They had left comfortable lives in France to make the dangerous sea journey and be among Montreal's first female European settlers.

▲ *This illustration shows Native Americans meeting with French settlers in the streets of Montreal in the seventeenth century.*

During the next two centuries, European demand for beaver pelts (used to make coats and hats) increased dramatically, and so did trade between Europeans and Indians. In 1611, the French soldier and scholar Samuel de Champlain visited the island of Montreal, and, in 1615, he returned there with two priests. Together they celebrated the first Catholic Mass in North America on Mont Royal. Champlain said, "I am here to bring about the Glory of God and the salvation of the Indians."

A Religious Mission
In 1642, a group of fifty French missionaries led by Paul de Chomedey founded the colony of Ville Marie de Mont Real (named

in honor of the Virgin Mary) on the island of Montreal. They began converting the Native Americans to Catholicism. These early French settlers were daring, spurred on by the belief that they were doing God's work. They were not welcomed by many of the Indians, however, and their tiny garrison was hit by many raids and ambushes.

Despite these frequent attacks, the settlement at Ville Marie flourished. The wealth generated by the fur trade brought more people, including the "Filles du Roi" ("daughters of the King")—young women transported from France to Ville Marie,

between 1664 and 1673, to marry the male settlers. Most were married within two weeks of arriving. These women shared the hardships of the settlers, including river flooding, poor crops, and long winters. While Ville Marie's population grew slowly, its fur trade boomed. During the next 150 years, furs were to become the area's most important source of wealth.

▼ *This illustration shows the death of General Montcalm, supreme commander of the defense of Quebec against the English. Like General Wolfe, Montcalm was fatally wounded on September 13, 1759, at the Battle of Quebec City.*

Fur Fairs

Canada's fur trade exploded because of a British fad for men's beaver hats. The hats needed to be treated with mercury, a poison, in a process that often made the hat-makers ill and gave rise to the phrase "mad as a hatter." Annual fur fairs were held in Montreal. A visiting Englishman named George Taylor, from Sheffield, arrived in Montreal in 1768 to find " the town very full of people from the remotest parts of the northern provinces, Indians that came 1,800 miles."

The Defeat of the French

In 1701, peace was finally achieved between the French and the Iroquois Indians. In 1710, Montreal dropped the name of Ville Marie and concentrated on becoming a trading center. Montrealers, however, did not relax their guard. In 1716, they began to build 18-foot (5.5-meter) stone walls around the town to protect against intruders.

In 1756, armed conflict, which became known as the Seven Years' War, broke out between the French and the British. Eager to make inroads into North America and the riches it promised, the British massed their forces. In 1759, they defeated the French army on the Plains of Abraham near Quebec City. On hearing that the French were fleeing, the victorious but mortally wounded British commander, General James Wolfe, murmured: "God be praised. Since I have conquered, I will die in peace."

Under British Control

In 1760, the French surrendered the city peacefully, and the British occupied Montreal. Despite these huge changes, daily life remained much the same for Montrealers. The British allowed them to retain their civil law and did not interfere with the teachings of the Roman Catholic Church. During the American Revolution (1775–83) Montreal was occupied briefly by American troops who felt sure that the city would be glad to be freed from British control. Montrealers, however, seemed happy and prosperous under the British. The disillusioned American revolutionaries finally withdrew in 1783.

Commercially, the city boomed. French, English, and Scottish residents lived and traded alongside one another. The British inhabitants also intermarried with French Canadians and seemed happy living in a city still essentially French. However, for two centuries, commerce in Montreal was run by the British inhabitants, while the French Canadians did the lower-paid work. Scottish explorers and merchants such as Simon Fraser, Alexander Mackenzie, Simon McTavish, and William McGillivray all made their mark on Montreal. In 1783, a group of them set up the North-West Company. This fur-trading organization challenged the position of the leading fur trader, the English-owned Hudson's Bay Company, which also had its headquarters in Montreal.

The railroad came to Montreal in 1853. Some years later, in 1867, modern Canada was created by the British North America Act, which joined together Nova Scotia, New Brunswick, Ontario, and Quebec. In 1886, the Canadian Pacific Railway was opened between Montreal and western Canada. By the 1890s, Montreal was Canada's only metropolis with a population of more than 200,000. It was also the major port and the eastern terminus of a cross-Canada rail route.

Century of Wealth

Sir Wilfred Laurier, Canada's popular Quebec-born prime minister, predicted that the twentieth century would belong to Canada. In the early decades of the century, the statement certainly applied to Montreal; with its busy rail yards and its port full of ships loaded with grain for overseas, the city became the country's center for finance.

Prosperity for the few was generally at the expense of increasing numbers of impoverished immigrants flooding in from places such as Ireland, eastern Europe, China, Greece, Portugal, and Italy. As the population grew to more than 500,000, the old, moneyed, English-speaking families of Montreal retreated into their exclusive estates in Westmount, on the western slope of Mont Royal.

Old Quarrels

With a British minority still largely in control of the city's economy, the old divisions between British and French widened farther. Many French Canadians were in favor of fighting on Britain's side in the two world wars of the twentieth century. However, the Québécois men of Montreal (French-Canadians who believed in independence from Britain) objected to the draft, and some openly opposed it. French-speaking Canadians began to make their voices heard on the political scene.

◄ *Sir Wilfred Laurier served as Canadian prime minister from 1896 to 1911.*

The Botanic Garden

In 1929, during the Great Depression, Montreal Mayor Camilien Houde listened while Brother Marie-Victorin, a priest and renowned botanist, publicly said: "We will soon be celebrating Montreal's three hundredth birthday. You need to give a royal gift to the city. But Montreal is a woman . . . and you certainly can't give her a storm sewer or police station. It is obvious what you must do. Fill her arms with all the roses and lilies of the field."

Mayor Houde helped relieve the city's serious unemployment situation by enlisting two thousand people to create a botanic garden. Today, only Kew, in England, is bigger. Montreal's garden has 22,000 plant species planted in rose, formal, herb, and vegetable gardens. There are Chinese and Japanese pavilions, an arboretum, an insectarium, and giant greenhouses for winter visitors.

The Quiet Revolution

Maurice Duplessis, the premier of Quebec province following World War II, used to argue against allowing "alien capitalists" into the province. Duplessis found he could exercise political control most effectively if he kept Quebec isolated. His government took advantage of the power wielded by the Roman Catholic Church, which, combined with his efforts, helped to keep many rural communities in ignorance and poverty.

A National Hero

Pierre Trudeau was born in Montreal in 1919 to a Québécois father and a Scottish mother. After graduating in law at the University of Montreal, he rose to become prime minister of Canada between 1968 and 1984 and was arguably the country's most brilliant and popular leader. Trudeau favored a bilingual Canada and worked subtly to undermine the Québécois separatist movement. He died on September 28, 2000, at the age of eighty. His state funeral, at Notre-Dame Basilica in Old Montreal, was the largest in Canada's history.

▲ *Prime Minister Pierre Trudeau (center) leaves the House of Commons in Ottawa after a Parliament meeting to discuss FLQ terrorist attacks in 1970.*

A new liberal feeling, brought about by something called the Quiet Revolution of the 1960s, helped change this and politicized the people of Montreal. The role of the church was challenged, and economic and social reforms soon followed.

Quebec's rich natural resources—hydroelectric power, uranium, and timber—became more valuable than ever on the world markets, and Canadian people began to enjoy greater prosperity. There was a new openness; women were considered men's equals, and huge families were no longer thought of as the norm. In the universities and cafés, the notion of an independent Quebec became a hot topic for discussion.

In 1968, a new provincial political party called the Parti Québécois (PQ) was formed. Its leader was the dynamic politician and journalist René Lévesque. The PQ was determined to bring the matter of independence for Quebec to a vote. It did not believe that the culturally French province should belong to a federation that was forcing it to become English.

Terrorism
On October 5, 1970, a radical group called the Front de Libération du Québec (FLQ) kidnapped James Cross, a British diplomat (he was eventually released). Five days later, the FLQ kidnapped Pierre Laporte, the Quebec labor minister. His body was found two weeks later.

During the 1970s, the FLQ carried out a letter-bombing campaign, injuring ordinary Montrealers and soldiers and blowing up mail boxes. The FLQ's slogan was "Independence or Death!" Eventually Prime Minister Pierre Trudeau sent federal troops to Montreal and other Quebec cities to guard government officials.

"We are nothing more than an internal colony, which lives at the will of another people."

—René Lévesque, founder of the Parti Québécois, on the subject of the French-speaking minority in Canada.

The troops were withdrawn in January 1971, after police arrested four members of the FLQ and charged them with the kidnapping and murder of Laporte. Many Canadians said it was Trudeau's finest hour. Many Québécois hated him. The action halted terrorism in Montreal, but it did not prevent the rise to power, in 1976, of the Parti Québécois.

Independence
In 1980, a referendum on the issue of independence for Quebec was voted down, but the powerful British minority in Montreal were still concerned. They began moving their businesses—and their jobs—to Toronto.

In recent years, the Parti Québécois has realized that, economically, Quebec cannot thrive alone. Quebec has begun to demand an increased participation in the Canadian federation. Latest estimates show that 75 percent of French-speakers have a working knowledge of English, while most English-speakers have mastered French. Montreal, as ever, is a city in which many of the differences are fought and, occasionally, settled.

CHAPTER 2

People of Montreal

The people of Montreal possess a "joie de vivre"—enthusiasm for life. They are passionate about good food, fashionable clothes, entertainment, and sports, and especially about their city. French Canadians are by far the largest group of people in Montreal. After the end of World War II, however, hundreds of thousands of immigrants from Europe settled there, followed, more recently, by immigrants from China and Haiti.

The French majority in Montreal speaks French and expects everyone else to do the same. These Montrealers are protective of their French way of life. Elsewhere in Canada, French and English are recognized as official languages—but not in Montreal. Here, local laws dictate that French is the official language for business and government. Signs throughout the city appear mainly in French.

The Two Solitudes

While the French- and English-speaking communities in Montreal have nearly always lived together peacefully, they remain distinct, parallel societies. They have never grown together and remain to this day "the two solitudes." Each has its

◀ *A street violinist entertains locals and tourists. Live acoustic music is hugely popular among the people of Montreal.*

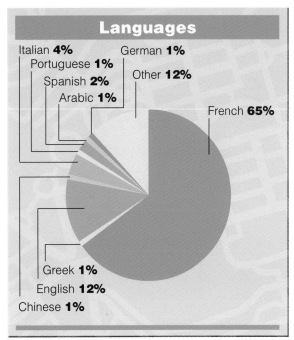

Languages

- Italian **4%**
- Portuguese **1%**
- Spanish **2%**
- Arabic **1%**
- German **1%**
- Other **12%**
- French **65%**
- Greek **1%**
- English **12%**
- Chinese **1%**

▲ *Montreal's Chinatown is packed with shops and restaurants and is generally busiest on weekends.*

own schools, colleges, universities, hospitals, newspapers, theaters, and business communities. Montreal's economy was once controlled by private companies that used English as the language of business. As a result, Montrealers needed to speak English to get a well-paying job. In 1977, however, the Quebec government ordered that companies employing more than fifty people should use French as the language of business. This means that there is no longer the great wage gap—French managers are as widespread as English managers—and many of Canada's largest international companies are owned by French-speakers from Montreal.

Despite the cultural differences, Montreal's population is cosmopolitan. Like English-speakers, French-speaking Montrealers watch Hollywood movies and TV soap operas. They buy English-language magazines. In other words, Montreal's French-speakers, like its English-speakers and even those people whose native tongue

"Joual"

English-Canadians used to argue that "Quebec French" was not worth learning because it was not pure "Parisian French." The Québécois dialect was called "joual," after the way that French-speaking Montrealers pronounced the word "cheval" (horse). Joual was the dialect of the city's working class and can still be heard, but it is less common than it used to be. Today, more than half of Montrealers are bilingual (speak both French and English), and some are trilingual (speak three languages).

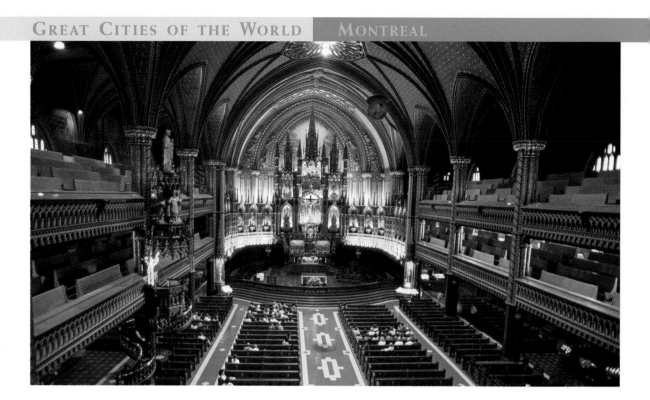

▲ *Notre-Dame Basilica in Old Montreal has a glittering interior, which includes intricate woodcarving and a blue-and-gold painted nave.*

is neither French nor English, are finding that their cultural boundaries are dissolving. The French spoken in Montreal often uses English expressions, an example of which is the all-purpose greeting: "Hi-bonjour."

The Ethnic Mix

Montreal has vibrant ethnic communities, the oldest and largest of which are Italian and Jewish. About 3 percent of the city's population is Jewish. The various newer ethnic groups—for example, Chinese, Greek, Vietnamese, Haitian, and Lebanese—have transformed the face of the city. Haitians operate many of the taxi companies, and Chinese and Greek people run most of the fast-food restaurants.

Different Faiths

Roman Catholics (mostly of French descent) make up about four-fifths of the city's population. The majority of English-speaking Montrealers are Protestants. Montreal has more than three hundred churches. Many French-speaking Catholics attend Montreal's most famous church, Notre-Dame Basilica in Old Montreal. St. Patrick's Church in downtown serves the English-speaking Catholic community. There are Jewish synagogues in the Hampstead and Outremont areas.

The Sailors' Church

Notre Dame de Bonsecours is another well-known church near the waterfront in Old Montreal. Some Montrealers call it "the sailors' church" because its belfry lantern guided mariners on their journey up the St. Lawrence. Its ceiling is hung with model

"This is the first time I was ever in a city where you could not throw a brick without breaking a church window."

—Mark Twain, American author and commentator, 1881, remarking on the extraordinary number of churches (74 in 1874) in Montreal. By 2004, the number had risen to more than three hundred.

ships, and a statue of the Virgin Mary on its roof has outstretched arms to welcome travelers into port.

The Cathedral-Basilica of Mary, Queen of the World, is in the heart of downtown. The designers of this church modeled it on St. Peter's Basilica in Rome. The Protestant Christ Church Cathedral, designed by Frank Wills of Salisbury, England, is also in downtown Montreal.

The huge dome of St. Joseph's Oratory, on the green northwest slopes of Mont Royal, is what first stands out for air travelers flying into Montreal International Airport at Dorval, southwest of the city. The oratory attracts more than three million visitors a year and can accommodate up to twelve thousand people at a time.

A Special Day

As long ago as 1834, the Canadian journalist Ludger Duvernay was concerned that the French-speakers were losing their identity. He formed societies throughout Quebec province, choosing John the Baptist as a patron saint. Eventually, St.-Jean-Baptiste Day was made a holiday in Quebec.

▲ *The St.-Jean-Baptiste Day parade is an example of how Montrealers like to party.*

The St.-Jean-Baptiste Day parade, held on June 24, is Montreal's biggest. The day, now officially called the "la fête nationale," has become a more important holiday than Canada Day (July 1). During the 1970s, when the Quebec separatist movement was at its height, the parade was dominated by political propaganda. Now, it is very much a multicultural family affair, with floats, bands and blue-and-white, fleur-de-lis provincial flags. This flag is more commonly seen in Quebec than is the maple leaf flag of Canada.

▲ *A typical restaurant on Rue Saint-Denis offers outside dining in warm months.*

Two Special Dishes

"Tourtiere" is a ground pork pie, heated and served after Midnight Mass in Quebec homes on Christmas Eve. There are many variations of this old dish, some with added potatoes, others with onions, peppers, herbs, or brandy. A Montreal newspaper's food editor found 58 different recipes.

Unlike tourtiere, "poutine" is rarely found outside the province. That is because people either hate it or love it. Mainly served at roadside stands on styrofoam plates, it consists of french fries smothered in gravy and topped with cheese curds.

Glorious Food!

Ask a Montrealer what is his or her favorite pastime, and the answer is likely to be "eating out." In North America, the city ranks with New York and San Francisco as a city where people can find gourmet food.

There are at least four thousand eating places to choose from. These range from bistros (where the variety of wines, beers, and soft beverages is as important as the food) to classic French restaurants, where dinner can cost close to $300 for two people. There are also American-style fast-food outlets, food courts in shopping malls, roadside stands and wagons selling french fries and "poutine" (*see box*), delicatessens, cafés, and small, ethnic restaurants.

Giant delis, such as Ben's, Dunn's, and Schwartz's, were, until recently, magnets for people seeking corned beef on rye bread. These Jewish-run outlets also sell Montreal smoked meat, a local specialty. Today, however, Montrealers are increasingly health conscious, and most tend to eat lighter meals.

Pea-soupers

The wives of the first French settlers canned fruits and vegetables and made soups at harvest time. Indeed, pea soup was such a favorite that the Québécois were known as "pea-soupers."

Even today, Montrealers use recipes handed down through the generations to prepare large family meals for weekends and holidays. Ingredients include the dairy products for which Quebec is renowned, together with fresh vegetables, maple syrup, local apples, top-quality beef from Alberta, salmon, scallops, and other seafood from both of Canada's coasts. These are often bought at Atwater Market, the biggest of Montreal's several markets.

Nowadays, with most people working, eating out is the rule rather than the exception. Montrealers can pick up a morning coffee and muffin at a drive-through Canadian chain, and get a fast take-out dinner on the way home.

For specialty eating places, Montrealers head to three areas: Old Montreal, the Latin Quarter, and the grid of downtown north and south streets, especially Crescent. Among the eighteenth- and nineteenth-century stone buildings, Old Montreal's

▲ Smoked meat at Schwartz's, the famous Jewish delicatessen on Boulevard Saint-Laurent.

small restaurants reflect the traditional French cuisine. Rue Saint-Denis, stretching beyond the Latin Quarter and around the University of Quebec at Montreal, attracts those looking for the menus of Vietnamese, Italian, and Greek chefs. Once the working day is over, the downtown grid is the place businesspeople go.

CHAPTER 3

Living in Montreal

Montreal is built on a series of terraces that rise from the banks of the St. Lawrence River west to Mont Royal. Old Montreal, with its historic houses and narrow cobbled streets, lies on the lower terraces, near the riverfront. The Boulevard Saint-Laurent, in downtown Montreal, is the historical east-west dividing line of the city. For many years, the French lived east of Saint-Laurent, and the English lived to the west. Montrealers still refer to the sections of the city as the East End and the West End.

During the early part of the twentieth century on Saint-Laurent, Moishe's and Schwartz's delis sold smoked meat and steaks at low prices. There were cheap movie houses, Jewish clothing stores, and pawnshops. To the west were wealthy homes, department stores, skyscrapers, and tourist attractions. To the east were factories, taverns, and "walkups," buildings with steep iron stairs on the outside, leading to balconies with railings. Here families would gather to play, gossip, and sun themselves.

Changes on The Main

All that has changed considerably. With successive waves of immigrants, Saint-

◀ *The Boulevard Saint-Laurent, or "The Main," has an incredibly varied ethnic and cultural mix. The area is full of interesting bookstores, second-hand clothes shops, bars, and restaurants.*

Laurent—nicknamed "The Main"—has expanded into a busy commercial district. It has become a mixture of expensive and affordable shops and cafés. The old slums to the east have been pulled down and replaced by rows of townhouses and detached three-bedroom homes. Saint-Laurent, however, is charming because many of the older shop fronts have been maintained rather than demolished.

Montreal has fewer family houses and more apartment buildings than any other Canadian metropolitan area. Nearly 70 percent of Montrealers lived in rented dwellings. Large numbers of the French rent apartments in the East End, but an increasing number are buying homes in the western suburbs, where there is an English-speaking majority.

The Suburbs

The "two solitudes" are most clearly shown by the areas in which the wealthy residents of Montreal still live. The two municipalities of Westmount and Outremont flank the Parc du Mont Royal and were started because some people wanted to escape the crowded and dirty conditions of nineteenth-century city living. Westmount is 80 percent English speaking, while Outremont is 80 percent French speaking. Both areas have fine houses, leafy parks, and busy commercial districts. Farther west, the former municipalities of Lachine and Beaconsfield have pleasant family dwellings with gardens, shops in local malls, and busy sports arenas.

The Writer's View

Montreal has produced a steady stream of authors, poets, and songwriters. In poetry, two Jewish-Canadian writers, Irving Layton and Leonard Cohen, were both born in Montreal and found the city inspired their world-famous verse and songs. It is the prolific author Mordecai Richler, however, who is both a Jewish-Canadian writer accused of being anti-Jewish, and a Montrealer accused of being anti-French, who has had the widest audience. His play, Jacob Two-Two Meets the Hooded Fang, is a young people's favorite.

"To a middle-class stranger . . . one street would have seemed as squalid as the next. On each corner a cigar store, a grocery and a fruit man. Outside staircases everywhere. Winding ones, wooden ones, rusty and risky ones. . . . An endless repetition of precious peeling balconies and waste lots. But, as the boys knew, each street . . . represented subtle differences. No two stores were the same, either. Best Fruit gypped on the scales, but Smiley's didn't give credit."

—From The Apprenticeship of Duddy Kravitz by Mordecai Richler.

Comfort Shopping

Downtown Montreal lies west of Old Montreal and has some of Canada's tallest buildings, busiest department stores, and finest hotels.

In the 1960s, Montreal became the first city in North America to "winterize" itself. It achieved this with the construction of a shopping mall underneath the main plaza of Place Ville-Marie. This subterranean mall is now linked under the streets of Montreal to many other plazas and the city's subway, or Métro. The whole system stretches 15 miles (24 km), with indoor entrances to 40 office towers, 10 downtown hotels, 1,600 shops, 1,200 businesses, 40 banks, 30 movie theaters, and hundreds of restaurants.

In this way, hundreds of thousands of Montrealers spend all day cocooned from the freezing Canadian winter outside. An office worker can travel by subway without

▲ *An underground shopping mall at Place Ville-Marie.*

a coat on the coldest day in January, arrive below his or her office building, take an elevator, work for the morning, descend to a concourse for lunch, get a haircut, return to work, then shop in the concourse before returning home by subway.

Shopping above Ground

There are normal, above-ground shopping streets in Montreal, too. The main ones are Rue Sherbrooke and Rue Sainte-Catherine. Both run east to west, about one-half mile apart. Rue Sainte-Catherine is a mix of major department stores, discount outlets, movie theaters, and souvenir shops. The department stores in downtown Montreal have equally large units in suburban shopping plazas near the metropolitan expressway across the city.

For everyday shopping, Montrealers still rely on the "corner store" for milk and other frequently used items, and the local baker for fresh baguettes. They do their weekly shopping in a supermarket.

Schools

Montreal has an unusual school system, organized on the basis of language and religion. There are four kinds of schools in the public school system: Roman Catholic schools that teach in English; Roman Catholic schools that teach in French; Protestant English-language schools; and Protestant French-language schools. Most Jewish-Canadian students attend either the Protestant schools or private Jewish schools.

Until the 1960s, education was controlled by the Roman Catholic Church. It was discovered, however, that Montreal's standards lagged far behind other Canadian cities. In 1964, a Ministry of Education was created in Montreal, and reform started. Today, in tests of reading, writing, and math in primary schools, Montreal pupils are at about the national average.

A Handsome Street

The stately Rue Sherbrooke sweeps through Montreal, dominating the city. This is perhaps fitting because, one hundred years ago, the 25,000 people living around its downtown area were reputed to control 70 percent of all Canada's wealth.

Wealth remains in this part of town. On Sherbrooke there is the Ritz Carlton Hotel, which, after ninety-two years, still serves as Montreal's most elegant establishment. There are also several other expensive hotels, the Museum of Fine Arts, private art galleries, the main campus of McGill University, the McCord Museum of Canadian History, famous name boutiques (like Cartier's) in the ground floors of nineteenth-century buildings, and office towers, their entrances enhanced by modern sculpture. Sherbrooke has the air of a Parisian boulevard, with tree-lined streets leading uphill off its north side and nestling against "the mountain."

Since the 1960s, the language in which education is provided has been a hot topic. In 1976, the Parti Québécois came to power and limited the teaching of subjects in the English language, much to the dismay of most English-speakers. Following the defeat of the Parti Québécois during the 1980s, compromises were reached: for example, today English-speaking schools receive the same financial support as French-speaking ones. Credits are now required in English to graduate from French-speaking schools, just as they are required in French to graduate from English-speaking schools.

Colleges and Universities

A major change in the 1960s was the introduction of junior colleges known as CÉGEPS (pronounced "say-jeps" by French-speakers and "see-jeps" by English-speakers). CÉGEP stands for Collège d'Éducation Générale et Professionelle. There are nineteen French-speaking colleges and four English-speaking. They run two-year courses, which prepare students for university entry. They also provide technical training.

Montreal has four universities. McGill University, founded in 1821 and situated along Rue Sherbrooke, is famous throughout North America partly because the humorist and author Stephen Leacock taught there, and also because Sir William Osler, the greatest of Canadian physicians, headed its medical faculty. At McGill and at Concordia University, also on Rue Sherbrooke, subjects are taught in English. The University of Montreal, situated on the slopes of Mont Royal, is the largest university outside of France in which all courses are taught in French. The University of Quebec, on the Rue Sainte-Catherine in the heart of the city, also teaches its courses in French. It is situated in the Saint-Denis district—an area renowned for its bohemian atmosphere and numerous cafés—center of Montreal's active student scene.

There are also many privately run language schools and schools for business administration and computer sciences for young adults. The number of private primary and secondary schools is also growing.

Getting Around

Public transportation by way of the bus and Métro services in Montreal is clean, efficient, quiet, and comfortable. More than 140 daytime and 20 night-time bus routes connect with 65 Métro stations on four different lines, so traveling to work from the suburbs could not be easier. As major bus routes operate around the clock, Montrealers can celebrate into the night in town and return home at any hour.

Driving in Montreal is another matter. It can be nerve-wracking. Traffic is often heavy and occasionally reckless. Traffic signs are in French only, which poses a challenge to many visitors. Parking is difficult in the city center, and regulations, in the form of parking tickets, are enforced.

Bikes, Trains, and Planes

Many Montrealers, escaping cars, ride bikes in town, especially in the parks. A network of cycle paths covering 140 miles (225 km) snakes through the city. Favorite routes include Lachine Canal, the Seaway, and Parc du Mont Royal.

Canada's passenger train service, Via Rail, has its headquarters in the city, and the company offers many trains to Toronto and

▲ Students take time out from classes at McGill University campus.

Quebec City, as well as the rest of Canada. Amtrak, a U.S. train network, provides a daily train service between Montreal and New York City. Commuter services to and from the suburbs are efficient.

Air Canada also has its headquarters in Montreal. There are two airports serving

the city. Dorval International, 14 miles (22 km) to the west, handles domestic, U.S., and international flights. There are hourly flights to Toronto and Ottawa and daily flights to many European cities. In the 1970s, a second airport was built at Mirabel, 34 miles (55 km) northwest of the city. Mirabel International was not a success, however, because it was built too far out of the city. It now handles mainly charter flights from outside North America.

▲ *Montreal has more than 20 specialized cycle trails.*

Unemployment

Today, the old divisions over national identity and the threat from terrorism (*see page 15*) are less acute, but other urban problems have taken their place. In the early 1990s, Montreal had a high rate of unemployment (27.3 percent in 1995). Poverty was also a problem, with nearly one out of every four Montrealers living below the poverty line.

The Quiet Subway

Montreal's Métro, which opened in 1966, is one of the world's quietest subways; this is because the trains run on rubber tires. The Métro carries passengers between downtown and the outskirts of the city in less than twenty minutes. Berri, one of the busiest Métro stations, is the interchange for the most heavily used lines, and it serves the nearby University of Montreal at Quebec station. Some of the stations were individually designed by architects and painters. One has an underground chapel; another is decorated in stained glass. They link with miles of walkways in the Underground City, and, at their ground-level exit doors, with Montreal's bus routes. Métro use in Montreal is high because of difficult winter driving conditions and severe cold, downtown congestion, and expensive parking.

▲ The Métro in Montreal is clean, quiet, and efficient.

One way of providing work for the unemployed is through temporary or seasonal employment. For example, traffic jams are a daily headache for motorists who have to cross any of the fourteen bridges leading into the city. These are always worse in winter snowstorms—the cleanup from which costs the city millions of dollars annually. The unemployed are given seasonal work as street shovelers. They certainly need it: In the poorer East End of the city, the jobless rate remains higher than the national average—at about 9.5 percent.

Social Problems

Fifty years ago, Gabrielle Roy, in her novel *The Tin Flute* stunned Canadians with her description of the poverty in Saint-Henri, a rundown district of Montreal. Today the city slums have gone, but the jobless remain.

Montrealers, however, have a safety net. There is a range of welfare benefits they can claim, including medicare (health insurance), unemployment insurance, pensions, and special aid for the disabled. Lower-paid Montrealers are more concerned about the continuation of these social benefits than

▼ *A homeless person sleeps under a cart in the center of Montreal. Few panhandlers live outdoors in winter—the weather is just too harsh.*

almost anything else. Montreal has a higher-than-Canadian-average membership in unions, although the membership does not tend to vote for leftist parties.

The New Poor

The real poor today are school dropouts and single moms. They mostly take on what are known as "Macjobs"—working at the minimum wage of Can$7.45 (US$4.50) an hour for fast-food chains and supermarkets. As temporary workers, they do not receive welfare benefits. Many of them, and the older unemployed too, look to the charitable St. Vincent de Paul Society for help and buy second-hand clothes from thrift shops.

▲ *Police on the streets of Montreal.*

A Safe City?

Crime is often related to poverty, but, despite high unemployment, the last ten years in Montreal have been successful economically. The crime rate has fallen, especially for homicides and assaults. For half a century, Montreal has been one of Canada's safest cities. Public respect for the police is fairly high.

The most highly publicized crimes of recent years have involved biker gang battles, some of which led to convictions for murder. Canada's Criminal Code applies to all citizens. No matter how poor, cititzens are entitled to a lawyer in major cases, paid for by Quebec's "legal aid fund." All have the right to have court proceedings conducted in their own language.

The Big Owe

Mayors do not tend to be well known outside their own cities. Not so Jean Drapeau, Montreal's mayor between 1954 and 1986. All Canadians knew of him. When the 1976 Olympic Games were scheduled to be staged in Montreal, Drapeau hired a French architect to design a futuristic stadium. This extraordinarily ambitious project had a retractable roof, which rarely worked, and a curving tower, which was dangerous. When Drapeau was questioned about the soaring costs, he made a famous reply: "The chances of the Olympics losing money were the same as that of a man having a baby." Drapeau died in 1999, but Montrealers are still paying for the Olympics debt through their taxes. Locals originally called the stadium the "Big O" because of its circular shape, but, after 1976, it rapidly came to be referred to as the "Big Owe."

CHAPTER 4

Montreal at Work

Today, Montreal is an international city and Canada's chief transportation center, with strong trading links to the rest of the world. Positioned as it is on the St. Lawrence Seaway, the city is an important stopover point for ships sailing between the Great Lakes and the Atlantic Ocean. Serving one of the largest grain ports in the world, Montreal Harbor stretches for 15 miles (24 km) along the west bank of the St. Lawrence River. In a year, the docks receive about 3,000 ships and handle more than 23 million tons (21 million metric tons) of cargo.

Roads and Railroads

Montreal is served by more than ten major highways. The Trans-Canada Highway, which runs from coast to coast, runs through downtown Montreal 100 feet (30 m) underground.

The city is one of Canada's largest railroad centers. CN North America, a transcontinental rail line, has its headquarters in Montreal. CN carries freight east and west to the Atlantic and Pacific coasts. The headquarters of the International Air Transport Association and the International Civil Aviation Organization, which control the world's airline activities, are both in Montreal.

◄ *Montreal is an important financial center. This photo shows the banking district in downtown.*

▲ *Ships still dock at the old harbor in Montreal.*

Trade and Finance

More than 40 percent of Canada's financial companies are in Greater Montreal, where banks, credit organizations, savings firms, and other financial companies employ more than 90,000 people. The Bank of Montreal, founded in 1817, was Canada's first bank. The country's largest bank, the Royal Bank of Canada, has its headquarters in Montreal. The Montreal Stock Exchange, which opened in 1874, is the oldest in Canada.

Industry

Manufacturing is the main source of employment in the greater Montreal area. About one-quarter of Montreal's workers are employed in more than 7,000 factories, producing goods worth about $25 billion annually. Greater Montreal's main industries are the manufacture of transportation

Ski-Doos

Joseph-Armand Bombardier was only fifteen years old when he invented the first snowmobile. It was driven by a wooden propeller and did not handle well in the heaviest snowdrifts, so Bombardier improved his vehicle. Eventually he founded a company and was ready to market the Ski-Dog (which, because of a typographical error, became the Ski-Doo).

Today there are millions of Ski-Doos. They are used for recreation, and there is a snowmobile trail stretching almost from coast to coast across Canada. More importantly, however, they have made life easier for farmers, forest workers, and many rural dwellers, who depend on them to get around during the winter months. Bombardier is now one of Montreal's top companies, with fifty thousand workers. They also build medium-sized airplanes, subway cars for Europe, and railroad cars for the United States.

equipment (Montreal has an auto plant and an airplane assembly plant) and food processing. The chief products are beer, sugar, and canned goods. The area is also a major producer of chemicals, clothing, electrical machinery, electronic equipment, and fur products. Montreal's petroleum refineries produce about one-tenth of Canada's gasoline.

Major employers include Lavalin, an international engineering company; Molson's, a brewery; BCE (Bell Canada Enterprises), a giant in the technological field; and Hydro Quebec and Abitibi (electricity and forest products). All the companies have major contracts with U.S. buyers, and all have research and administration facilities in Montreal.

Beer and Shipping

In 1786, an Englishman, John Molson, started a brewery on the banks of the St. Lawrence. He also founded a small shipping line and eventually made a vast fortune, using part of his wealth to open the first theater and hotel in Montreal. The Molson name today graces a stadium, an ice hockey arena, and several university buildings. The slogan invented by Molson—"An honest brew makes its own friends"—can still be found on his family's beer bottles to this day.

▼ *This Montreal plant manufactures aircraft used to fight forest, oil platform, and urban fires.*

Expo '67

In 1967, the World's Fair drew 53 million visitors to Montreal. Expo '67 was an entertainment and economic triumph. Two islands in the St. Lawrence River—Île Sainte-Hélène and Île Notre-Dame—were transformed from green spaces into vibrant city parks. Sophisticated pavilions were built, including a dome that today houses the Biosphère, an environmental center. An amusement park called La Ronde was also built to great acclaim. Today it is even bigger and better and contains Le Monstre, one of the world's tallest roller coaster rides.

Other important employers include George Weston, whose grocery stores extend to the United Kingdom; Pratt and Whitney, the aircraft engine builders; and Desjardin retail stores. Montreal is also noted for its small businesses. The city is home to hundreds of companies with fewer than thirty employees.

Other Industries

Tourism in Montreal is a major moneymaker. While tourism has decreased recently across most parts of Canada—there are especially fewer U.S. tourists since the terrorist attacks of 2001—Montreal has seen no significant decline. Two hours by air from Chicago and an hour and a half from New York City, it is a favorite foreign destination for its U.S. neighbors.

▲ *The Biosphere, built originally for Expo '67, now houses interactive displays highlighting the ecosystems of the Great Lakes and the St. Lawrence River.*

Montreal is also a major medical research center. World-famous researchers, such as the neurosurgeon Dr. Wilder Penfield and Hans Selye, an expert on stress, have carried out their research at the Royal Victoria Hospital in central Montreal.

Government

Local government in Montreal is run by an elected council of fifty-six members headed by a mayor. The city council is elected for four years. The council selects a six-member executive committee, which proposes new laws and prepares the city's budget.

▲ *City Hall is the center of government in Montreal.*

The council passes the city's laws, agrees on the annual budget, and appoints and dismisses directors of city departments.

The city of Montreal has an annual budget of about $1.9 billion. More than 40 percent of Montreal's funds come from taxes on property. The rest come from taxes on sales, businesses, water, amusements, and funds given by Quebec province.

An agency called the Montreal Urban Community Council administers services such as fire protection, law enforcement, public health, public transportation, traffic control, sanitation, and water supply. Montrealers seem generally satisfied with their services, although they are faced with considerable delays for non-urgent medical treatment, as well as some merging of schools to save money, and cutbacks in other services.

Media and Communications

French-speaking Montrealers have a choice of three daily newspapers—*La Presse*, *Le Devoir*, and *Le Journal de Montreal*. The *Gazette*, founded in 1778 and therefore Montreal's oldest newspaper, is the only Montreal daily to be written in English.

There are seven French-language and eight English-language radio stations. Three television stations broadcast in French and two in English. The French-language network of the Canadian Broadcasting Corporation (CBC) is based in the city. Montreal produces more French-language television programs than any other city in the world, apart from Paris.

The Industry of Images

Quebec-made movies are popular within the province, and they are also well liked in France, Belgium, and French-speaking parts of Africa. Among them are My Uncle Antoine *(often judged the best movie ever made in Canada), movies with an ice hockey theme (always a box office draw), and historical movies such as* The Black Robe. *Quebec-born Denys Arcand, whose two greatest hits were* The Decline and Fall of the American Empire *and* Jesus of Montreal, *is the leading director in Canada.*

▼ *A selection of Montreal's newspapers reflects the city's primary languages.*

CHAPTER 5

Montreal at Play

A popular Canadian song begins with the words: "Winter, it's my country." Certainly, Montrealers long ago decided to welcome and celebrate winter rather than fight it. For ten days each February, the Fête des Neiges (Snow Festival) takes place on îles Notre-Dame and Sainte-Hélène. Montrealers mark this event by building giant snow castles, ice slides, and sculptures. They also compete in kite-skating, barrel-jumping, and dog sled or ice canoe racing.

Skiing and Other Activities

To the north of Montreal are the Laurentians, Quebec's highlands, consisting of deep woods, glacial lakes, and alpine villages. The Laurentians and the Estrie (to the east of the city) are the two main playgrounds for Montrealers. In the winter, two favorite pastimes for Montrealers are downhill and cross-country skiing, and today snowboarding is a major attraction for teenagers. Mont Tremblant, the premier Laurentians ski resort, is one of the top

"We do not fight winter. We invite it, play with it, welcome it."

—A Montreal resident.

◀ Children explore an ice sculpture at the Montreal Snow Festival, held annually on two islands in the middle of the St. Lawrence River.

three in North America. Its hiking trails, hotels, restaurants, and shops are typical of the area. Mont-Orford Park, in the Estrie, is popular in all seasons, providing cross-country skiing and skating in winter and hiking, golf, and hang-gliding in summer.

Montreal itself has a large range of indoor places in which to spend a winter's day. The Biodôme, the former Olympics bicycle racing stadium in the Parc Olympique, is now a living museum where visitors can see birds, animals, and plants in recreations of their natural habitats. Visitors can also pass through a tropical rain forest and polar region, and there is a miniature ocean, complete with nesting birds and tidal pools. The Canadian Center for Architecture contains models of famous buildings and is arguably the world's premier architectural museum.

Movies and Theater

Montreal is one of North America's leading cultural centers. It showcases outstanding dance, drama, and musical groups. The downtown Place des Arts has four concert halls offering ballet, opera, and, most particularly, weekly performances by the Montreal Symphony Orchestra. Montreal's principal ballet troupe is Les Grands Ballets Canadiens. Montrealers also enjoy movies, and there is an independent film festival that takes place in June, followed by the Montreal International Film Festival in August. Montrealers also have the choice of live theater from about forty

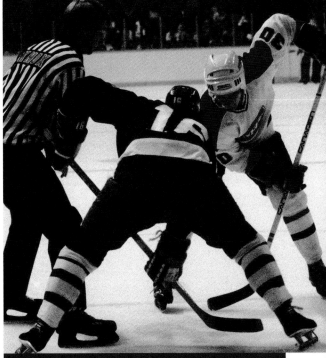

Hockey Fever

In Montreal, ice hockey is a passion. The Montreal Canadiens team has won the National Hockey League's championship Stanley Cup a record twenty-four times since 1929, and all Montreal follows the games of its favorite team between October and June each year.

Each season, Les Canadiens play about forty home games at the Molson stadium. Hockey is a rough but graceful, rowdy but rule-bound game. Canadians are among the best players in the world, and Montrealers are unquestionably among the most loyal fans.

French-language groups, and English-language productions at the Centaur Theater, a former stock exchange.

People Watching

In May, on the first warm day in the city, café owners spread red-and-white checkered cloths on tables outside. Montrealers take their coats off, sit down, order a croissant and "café au lait," and begin to indulge in another of their favorite activities—people watching. Montreal is Canada's fashion capital, and its men and women dress with great style. Montrealers are famous for their sophisticated tastes and are passionate about shopping; they love to parade the latest trends on downtown streets.

Montreal's best shopping areas are near the McGill Métro station and along Rue Sainte-Catherine. Many of the major department stores are in the Underground City (see page 24) and these sell designer label clothes at high prices, but there are cheaper shops in Old Montreal, for example on rues Notre-Dame and Saint-Jacques. The less conventional shoppers frequent The Main, where they can find bohemian clothing stores, bookstores, galleries, and antique stores.

Time Out

Many Montrealers take advantage of the good summer weather and spend weekends relaxing at lakeside cottages in the Laurentians. Many families enjoy visiting the Cosmodome in the suburb of Laval, a 30-minute drive from downtown. Here they can see replicas of rockets and spaceships, and a full-size mock-up of the space shuttle

Cirque du Soleil

The Cirque du Soleil (Circus of the Sun) has revolutionized the idea of what a circus should be. For a start it has no animals, no old-fashioned clowns, and no ringmaster. Started by Guy Laliberte, a Montreal street performer, it is a mixture of Broadway musical and futuristic spectacle. It delights audiences with amazing acrobats, original music, marvelous mimes, performers from around the world, humor, magic, and fantasy, and is the most successful arts show Canada has ever produced.

Every other summer a new production of the circus opens in Montreal. It stages performances in Quebec City and Toronto before moving on to the United States. There is also a different touring production in Europe, and there are two based permanently at Las Vegas and Orlando. From its headquarters in Montreal, the Cirque du Soleil also operates the world's leading circus school.

Endeavor. In the middle of town at the Old Port, now an entertainment complex, there is an Imax movie theater, an archeological museum, and a science center.

Adventurous Montrealers go whitewater canoeing and kayaking. They can also enjoy boat cruises on the river and jet ski thrills through the Lachine Rapids. There is boating, fishing, sailboarding, and para-sailing at Magog, near Mont Orford, east of the city.

▲ *Crowds gather around a band on stage at the Montreal Jazz Festival.*

Jazz and Other Festivals

During the summer, Montrealers can choose from a range of free concerts in the city parks. They can hear free organ recitals at St. Joseph's Oratory (*see page 19*). In July, the world's biggest jazz festival takes place at fifty-three sites, most of them open-air, and attracts one million people. Big-name performers like Wynton Marsalis take over large venues and local clubs for ticketed concerts, but other events are held outdoors and are free.

Also in July, for ten days, the "Just For Laughs" comedy festival, now in its twentieth year, brings its humor to town. Indoor and outdoor shows feature acrobats, street comedians, mime artists, and clowns. Guest performers have included Jerry Seinfeld, Joan Rivers, and Jay Leno.

Other events include a grand prix motor racing weekend on a track named after local racing driver hero Jacques Villeneuve; a food festival in August in which restaurants offer outdoor feasts on Île Notre-Dame; and an International Festival of New Dance, which features dancers and choreographers from around the world.

CHAPTER 6

Looking Forward

Today, Montreal is a multicultural city. Those with ethnic backgrounds other than French or English include Jews, Italians, Greeks, and many people from the Indian subcontinent, the Caribbean, and Africa. The result of this ethnic mix is a lively, stylish, and broad-minded city, whose population has an enthusiastic interest in a wide range of cultural activities.

The Canadian government is determined to increase the country's population by 1 percent a year (in other words, by about 350,000 people) through immigration. While new arrivals are encouraged to settle in smaller towns, the vast majority will probably continue to head for the cities. Montreal's newer communities will probably continue to be from Vietnam, Haiti, and French-speaking African countries, and they will continue to change the face of Montreal.

An Aging Population

Age is a problem in Montreal, as elsewhere in Canada. As the city's population grows older, the health costs increase. The average age of a citizen of Montreal is now thirty-seven, two years older than it was in 1996.

◀ In 1995, young Montrealers wave Canadian flags and demonstrate against the idea of a separate state for Quebec. Many young Canadians are now in favor of national unity.

▲ *A view of the city skyline of Montreal, looking across the St. Lawrence River.*

About 80 percent of people being treated in city hospitals are over the age of sixty-five. The city needs young people to work in its business and services. In the past, younger people tended to move to Montreal from some of the poorer Atlantic provinces of Canada. Now they tend to migrate to richer Alberta.

Investing in the City

Generally, though, the economic future looks bright for Montreal. Thirty years ago, when separatism was at its height and the future looked uncertain, American businesspeople were particularly unwilling to start branch plants in Quebec province. Although the arguments concerning the protection of the French language continue, it appears that there is no longer a huge groundswell of support for a separate Quebec. This means that there is more stability, and a greater willingness by outsiders to start businesses in Montreal. Younger people are more determined to get a technical or university education and to become fluent in a second language. Job opportunities are a high priority.

Like other big cities, Montreal has difficulty finding ways to pay for the rapidly rising costs of government services. In common with many Canadians, Montrealers are particularly concerned about health and the environment. Most Montrealers want money to be spent on improving these services, rather than on more police or increasing the armed forces.

The city has adopted a long-range urban development plan. Many of the development projects taking place in downtown Montreal focus on preserving its architectural heritage. Such projects should contribute to the world image of Montreal as a dynamic, international city, which takes pride in its past achievements while anticipating the future with hope and confidence.

Time Line

1535 French navigator Jacques Cartier reaches Hochelaga, an Indian village, later to become the site of Montreal. He names the hill above it Mont Royal ("Mount Royal").

1608 Samuel de Champlain establishes Quebec City, the first permanent settlement in Canada.

1611 A trading post called Place Royale near Hochelaga becomes the site of first settlement of Montreal.

1642 The first colonists, under Paul de Chomedey, a French soldier, establish a religious mission named Ville Marie de Mont Real, a permanent settlement that will grow into Montreal.

1759 The British, under General James Wolfe, defeat the French forces on the Plains of Abraham.

1760 The French surrender Montreal to the British.

1775–76 American revolutionaries, including Ben Franklin, arrive in Montreal and try unsuccessfully to convince Montrealers to join the American revolutionary cause against Britain.

1778 The first issue of the newspaper that will later become *The Montreal Gazette*, Montreal's only English-language daily, is published.

1821 McGill University opens.

1824 The Lachine Canal is opened, enabling ships to travel between the Atlantic and the Great Lakes.

1832 Montreal is officially made a city.

1852 Nine thousand people are left homeless after a fire destroys much of the city.

1867 The Dominion of Canada is formed, consisting of Quebec, Ontario, New Brunswick, and Nova Scotia.

1886 The newly completed Canadian Pacific Railway opens its line from Montreal to Vancouver.

1914–18 English and French Canadians are deeply divided over being drafted for service in World War I.

1924 On Christmas Day, a cross on Mont Royal is lit for the first time; it has been a landmark ever since.

1940–45 Most Montrealers oppose the draft to serve on the side of the Allies in World War II. Mayor Camilien Houde of Montreal is imprisoned for urging Canadians not to register for wartime conscription.

1959 The St. Lawrence Seaway opens, enabling oceangoing ships to travel into the heartland of the United States, as far as the Great Lakes and key ports such as Chicago.

1967 The Expo '67 World Fair attracts 53 million visitors.

1970 FLQ terrorists kidnap the British Trade Commissioner, James R. Cross, and Quebec Labor Minister, Pierre Laporte. Prime Minister Pierre Trudeau sends federal troops to Montreal. Laporte is murdered, but Cross is released.

1976 Summer Olympics are held in Montreal. Parti Québécois wins the provincial election.

1980 A vote for a separate Quebec province is narrowly defeated.

2002 All 24 municipalities on the island of Montreal are merged into one super-city.

Glossary

baguettes long, thin loaves of white bread.

brioches soft French pastries made from a very light yeast dough.

CÉGEP an abbreviation for Collège d'Éducation Générale et Professionelle, a type of junior college in Quebec, providing university preparation or trade training.

civil law the law of a state relating to private or civilian affairs.

colony a territory, overseas or abroad, that belongs to a state. Canada, for example, was once a British colony.

conscription compulsory military service.

constitutional monarchy a political system in which the monarch's powers, rights, and duties are limited and defined by law.

ecosystem a system involving the relationship between living creatures and their non-living environment.

federation a form of government in which several states give up certain powers to a central authority, but also have limited powers to run their own affairs.

Filles du Roi or "King's daughters"—1,000 young women who were paid to become early settlers of Ville-Marie de Montreal and other places in Canada.

flotilla a small fleet, or fleet of small ships.

garrison a fortified place, maintained and guarded by troops.

Lachine Rapids a navigational obstacle near Montreal; these rapids were named after China, the country that early explorers were seeking.

The Main the nickname for Boulevard Saint-Laurent, a street which marks the east-west dividing line of Montreal.

Métro Montreal's subway system.

missionaries people who are sent by a religious body, especially a Christian church, to a foreign country to do religious and social work.

nave the central space in a church.

patisserie the French word for bakery.

Quebec the largest of Canada's ten provinces. Montreal is the largest city in Quebec province.

rapids part of a river where the water flows very qickly.

retractable describes something that can be drawn in. For example, a retractable roof is a roof that can be drawn or folded back.

rue the French word for "street."

St. Lawrence River Canada's most important river. The St. Lawrence rises at Lake Ontario, flows 200 miles (321 km) to Montreal, and then 1,000 miles (1,600 km) to the Atlantic.

separatist someone who promotes withdrawal from an organization or group. The Quebec separatists promoted withdrawing their province from Canada.

Further Information

Books

Bowers, Vivien. *Wow! Canada.* Maple Tree Press, 1999.

Kalman, Bobbie, and Niki Walker. *Canada from A to Z.* Crabtree Publishing, 1999.

Klement, Alice. *Insight Pocket Guide to Montreal.* Insight Guides, 2002.

Landau, Elaine. *Canada.* Children's Press, 2000.

Little, Catherine, and Stephen Keeler. *What It's Like to Live in Canada.* Waterbird Press, 2003.

Rogers, Stillman D. *Montreal (Cities of the World).* Children's Press, 2000.

Roles, Julia. *Insight Guide to Montreal and Quebec City.* Insight Guides, 2001.

Symon, John. *The Lobsters Kids' Guide to Exploring Montreal.* Lobster Press, 2000.

Web Sites

www.montrealcam.com/webcam/biodome/webcam.jpg
Take a look at Montreal's biodome through its webcam.

www.easyexpat.com/montreal_en/overview_history.htm
Learn more about Montreal's history, language issues, and legislation.

www.cia.gov/cia/publications/factbook/geos/ca.html
Find detailed facts about Canada at a glance.

www.planetarium.montreal.qc.ca/
Gain both French and English access to Montreal's planetarium, and link to Montreal's biodome, insectarium, and botanical gardens.

www.montreal.com/tourism/sports.html
Get an overview of Montreal's sports teams here.

http://www.cirquedusoleil.com/CirqueDuSoleil/en/default.htm
Explore scenes, plots, music, and more in Cirque du Soleil on the internet.

Index

Page numbers in **bold** indicate pictures.